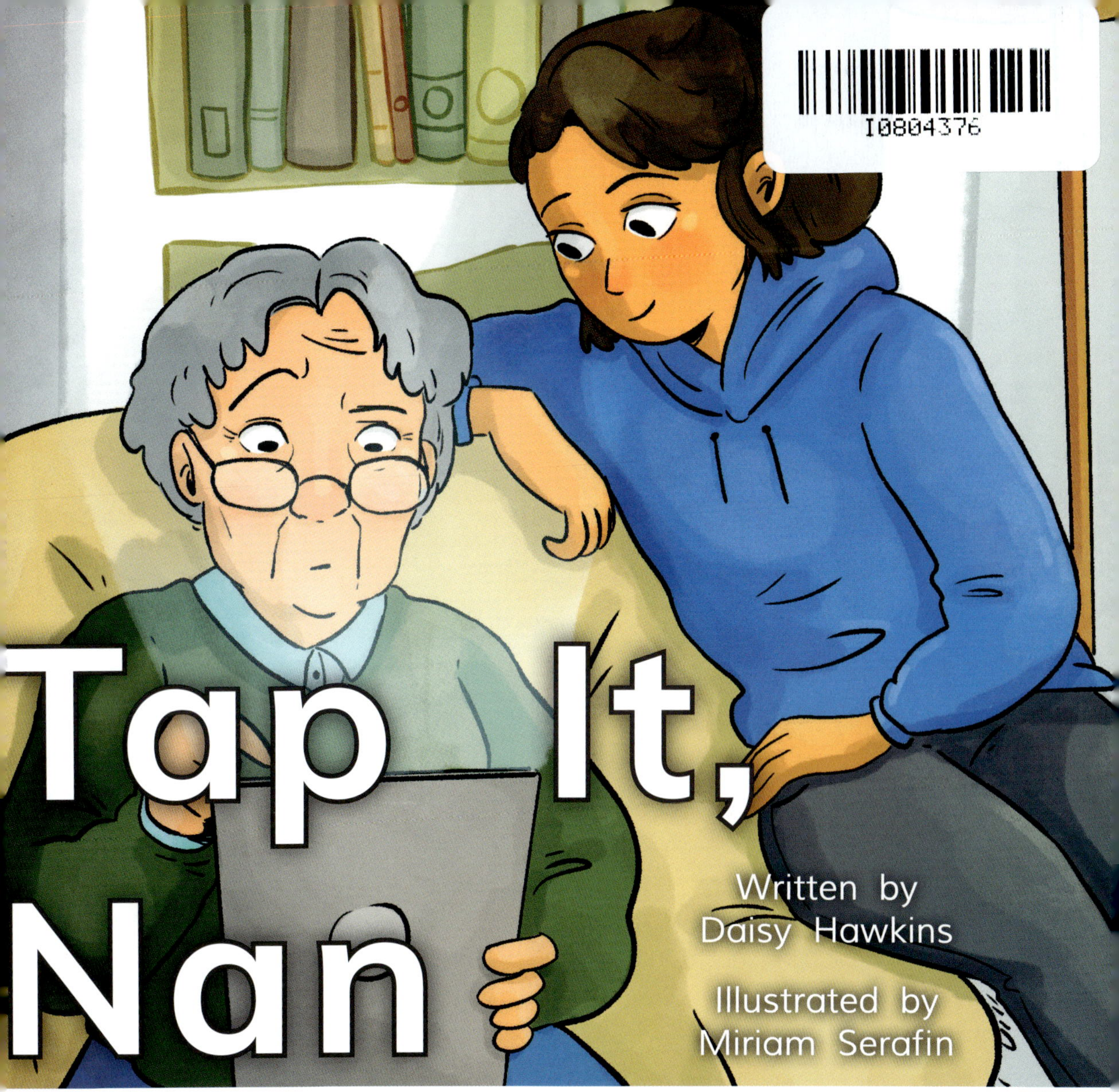

shed in 2026 by
wood House Press
4 Clinton Street
lo, NY 14224

d in the United States of America

Library of Congress Cataloging-in-Publication Data:
Names: Hawkins, Daisy, author. | Serafin, Miriam, illustrator. | Rix, Nicolas, illustrator.
Title: Tap it Nan / written by Daisy Hawkins, illustrated by Miriam Serafin. Tim did it / written by Daisy Hawkins, illustrated by Nicolas Rix.
Description: Buffalo, NY : Norwood House Press, 2026. | Series: Phonics all-stars: phase 2 |
Identifiers: ISBN 9781978577848 (pbk.) | ISBN 9781978577855 (library bound) | ISBN 9781978577862 (ebook)
Subjects: LCSH: Reading–Phonetic method–Juvenile literature. | English language–Phonetics–Juvenile literature. | Tablet computers–Juvenile literature. | Superheroes–Juvenile literature.
Classification: LCC LB1573.3 H395 2026 | DDC 372.465–dc23

CPSIA compliance information: Batch #CW26NHP: For further information contact Norwood House Press at 1-800-237-9932.

Pip!

Tap it,
Nan.

Pip!

Tip it,
Nan.

Pip!

Pin it,
Nan!

A nap,
Nan?

Tim Did It

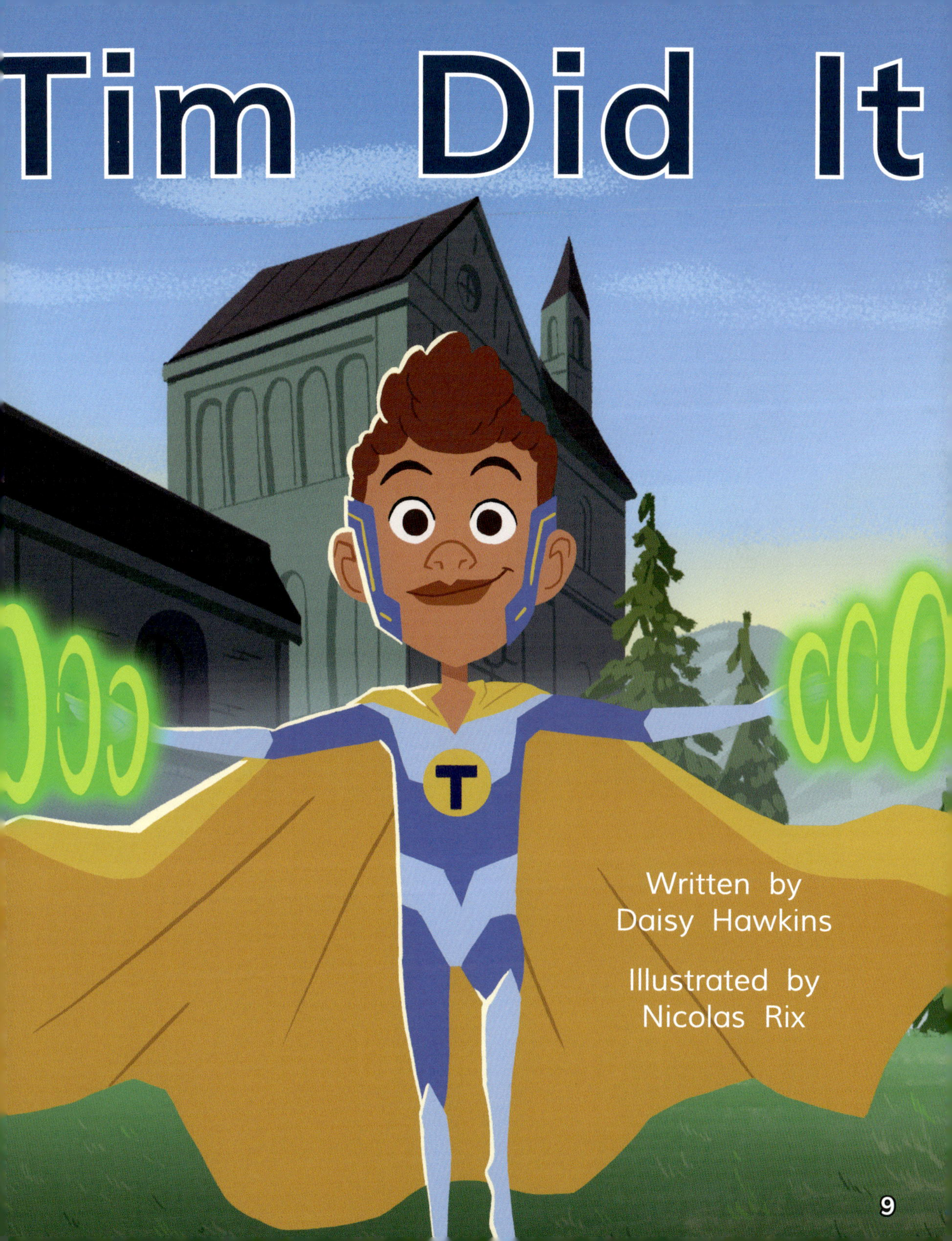

Written by
Daisy Hawkins

Illustrated by
Nicolas Rix

Pam did it.

Sid did it.

Mas did it.

Dan did it.

Pip did it.

Min did it.

Tim did it!